RECEPTIVE *Sentiments*

A POETRY CHAPBOOK

Nadia Benjelloun

AuthorHouse™ UK
1663 Liberty Drive
Bloomington, IN 47403 USA
www.authorhouse.co.uk
Phone: 0800.197.4150

Published by AuthorHouse 05/05/2015

ISBN: 978-1-5049-4135-8 (sc)
ISBN: 978-1-5049-4136-5 (e)

Print information available on the last page.

This book is printed on acid-free paper.

Contents

Introduction

My name-Nadia

When I think of my name, I think of soft creamy colour and dew.

I think of pearls and white roses too.

Love, hope and peace signs

Also come to my mind,

For my name does mean hope,

It is true I hardly mope,

My name is used in African, Arabic, Swahili, English and Russian speaking countries

I like to save many things, books, jewelry, useless old possessions that are valuable to me among other sundries.

In Slavic languages it is the Ukrainian word for hope

As well as in Russian,

It is the same in English, Bulgarian, and Persian.

Its origin is from Russia,

It is a diminutive form for Nadezhda,

Would you consider me as a person with some form of charisma?

At least is not, God forbid, stigma.

But in Arabic it means moist, delicate, tender,

Well, I don't usually lose my temper, for I do try to be patient since agitation is not something I'd want to engender,

Trying to be "good" –

Is a struggling awkward fight with the conscience,

But at least I tell myself I could,

And for the most part, I hope I am now somewhat understood.

Haikus

Light, emitting from

Center of the sun, where gold;

Center of life comes

Water

Colorless, no taste

Transparent, not aberrant

Very relied on

Darkness overcomes

Darkness overcomes.

O, fearful, dark, gloomy times,

Shall thy light come shine?

Free Verse

Little girl sat in the garden, to muse,

About random things,

Contingent things…

Birds chirping, the flowers dancing in the wind, the grass felt prickly.

Roses in

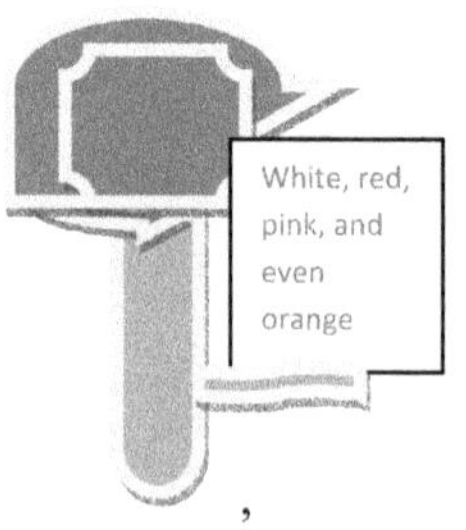

,

A beautiful aroma arised from them

That was the place of relaxation, the *time*, for genuine quiescence and serenity. The time.

Oh, but her relaxed sedentary

And mused state, was

Interrupted!

A daunting, black hound appeared out of nowhere

With eyes so black, you'd think they were pupils, wholly

Nay,

the iris black, and the pupils were red, revealing the dark secrets, and bloody evils out there-

that it witnessed, letting her know of the things it knew, things it did, things to beware.

Growling with its fang-like teeth, it s l o w l y approached. With sweat trickling down her back, she stood up,

Backed away.

But..

The sun still shined, and with eyes closed that was all gone. And *now*, as I open my eyes, I realize, I could always revisit that garden, be re-immersed in the bright part of it, and rejoice with that little girl.

If you did not get what I tried to imply,

That little girl,?..

It was I.

What Happens To a Dream Realized?

What happens to a dream realized?

Is it seized-

like the string of an inflated balloon with helium, that tried to escape into the air

Is it appeased-

Like an elderly who heard politeness from the generation they thought merely didn't care

Perhaps it simply allows those involved, to celebrate

And give those in the future, something new to anticipate

Yes, let that pair of arms swing and jubilate,

Let it be eulogized,

Like baby's first steps, child's first graduation, youth's first depart

Let it be panegyrized,

Everyone wants at least a piece of that dream whatever it takes, whatever it costs, fighting for, bargaining for it as a stamped of feet is at *that* mart

But Why,

Was it is because it had been like a shower down, after a successful prayer-rain dance,

Or made someone feel like they've finally owned, and live in a manse

Yes, this is how it is being materialized,

For this is what happens to a dream realized.

Baby Blue Eyes

Mesmeric golden light appeared out of the blue

An enticing, soft voice called out, “I’m here for you,”

Baby blue eyes, and deep brown coloured hair,

The eight year old girl really wanted to go there

To where the light seemed to beckon for her

Baby blue eyes ran across the purely green meadow

She felt a positive vibe run through her body as her skin begun to glow

Along the way were carnations, daisies and poppies that aligned together

In this meadow that seemed to stretch on forever

Upon seeing her favorite flowers, baby blue eyes
felt a supreme joy she never thought she

Could endeavor,

And there was a variety more, in different colour,

This was a dream, thought baby blue eyes,
for real-life flowers look duller

Suddenly, a loud blenching noise sounded from nowhere

It takes in baby blue eyes like a vacuum, to another memory; elsewhere

It was cold in the air, and the uncomfortable
and tense atmosphere was unfamiliar

as the contents of the meadow were replaced by stoneware.

Her eyes were closed, and she had no control over her body

She tried to call to the hushed murmurs she heard
around her, but her voice was drawly

A heart monitor beeped away

Baby blue eyes guessed this isn't a place where she'll be gay

A strong dominant voice repeatedly said, "Do
something! Do anything that'll save her!

No! rebelled every aching fiber of baby blue eyes

Can't you see I'm in convulsion?

Where is my dream? I want to go back. My
eyes are closed but I am not asleep.

Let me go back to where I felt as light and free as a soul

Instead of feeling the languish where I here thole

From this pain I'd like to acquit

Let me sleep. Let me rest. At least for a little bit.

Numb and in pain, baby blue eyes pleaded silently,

until a voice responded solemnly,

… " There's nothing that could be done"

A certain beeping came to a stop; the machine echoed its last one,

That being the last of what baby blue eyes heard,
before reopening her eyes to the ravishing

Golden light

Alas, she was back

Away from where it was dark and black

Elated, baby blue eyes skipped through the
meadow, getting ready to play,

Stronger and more beautiful than ever, the welcoming
womanly voice from the horizon said,"

this time you are here to stay"

Spirit

Child and adult are looking through a one-way window

On the other side of the empty room, lies a still body.

It was an adolescent girl whose eyes were half-open.

Her expression was emotionless.

Her almond loose hair lay across the floor in waves, as if it had been braided multiple times.

Her matching eyes were fixed, glaring at the ceiling, not dare moving, nor did they blink once.

Her skin as pale as ghost. She might as well have been frozen. Had it not been for the slow rise and fall of her chest, one would have thought she was dead.

"Is she alive?" the child asks.

"Yes." Responds adult.

"But how? She's barely moving."

"Look closer" adult points to the center of the room.

About a meter above the body, was another body, floating in the air in parallel.

It was exactly the same copy of the girl, only in a form of an apparition.

Transparent, and dressed in dull colors, the apparition looked even more lifeless.

It was visible that, on its back was a wire cord. The extension of the cord hung towards the ground, going downwards to the body below it.

And the other end of it was seemingly plugged into the girl's chest.

"What is it? A phantom?" asks child.

"Her spirit" answers adult.

"Why does it look so ghostly?"

"It's in a fragile state. Either the girl believes there isn't much to hold it down, or she herself is in a fragile state. I mean there's only a single cord that connect the two's life line. And a very thin one, I may add."

"So what's keeping her alive?"

"Whatever makes up her spirit."

"What makes up a spirit?"

"Depends on each one."

"What about her?"

"Observe." Adult points back at the window.

As if on cue, the spirit started wavering, making airy ripples through its structure.

Then it started to fade, shrink, and change shape.

The tip of the chord that had been connected to its back, cut open, and split into a couple of additional wires.

The spirit disappeared and was then replaced with several flying objects, each attached to the newly produced wires. All were still part of the same single chord between them and the body on the floor.

One of the objects was a book. Another was simply a comic book. The child wondered why they floated separately, and why couldn't they have been represented as one thing.

On another wire was a single, blank piece of paper with a pencil stuck on its surface.

The fourth object was three dimensional.

"What is that?" the child points towards it.

"It's a diorama of a bedroom." Explains the adult. Next to it floated a silver key.

The last object was a CD.

The child lastly says, "I think I now understand…"

Coming into Existence

Birth...

How did it come to be?

A black surface is visible,

One with an undetermined dimension,

and with an unknown texture.

But certainly not structured in the form of a volution.

And lain across it, are beings that will each be perceived as a treasure.

Little embryo-like figures-just lying there like pebbles.

A long, black, flowing cloak slides across the surface,
slithering and moving in between and around each one,

All either a future daughter or son.

When one has been selected, the cloak slides
itself underneath it like a spatula,

And wraps its covers of destiny around it.

Suddenly a golden light is emitted, and all the cosmos
are visible on the cover, all the stars, and components
of nebulae running through it like a screen.

Then soil starts gathering from an unknown source. Along
with it, turf is attracted to the bundled being like a magnet,
and creates a structure similar to a basket underneath it.

An opening is made in the direction above It,
and bright white light shines from it.

The soon-to-be-child is levitated, and taken towards it.

Through it, It goes,

and into the realm of Earth

to where it will then undergo Birth…

Who is he?

Who is he?

Who he? Oh, that guy, well he's nobody.

No, that's not the person, I know, he's full of probity.

Well he can't be much of anything else, to the likeness of
others- indifferent, and always wandering around alone,
never seen him hanging out or eating lunch with anybody

Well that can't be so, have you seen him at the winter break party?
Seems to me like a different person to the one you're describing-

Was greeted everywhere, laughing his head off with a crowd of
friends, cool, charismatic and seemingly with a great sense of humor

Well then, you must be mistaken, he's socially awkward,
cloistered, humble, and extremely timid, couldn't see
him interacting as you say, probably can't even handle
something challenging in life-nothing but an underdog

Seems to me, within premises of your high school, he's just a cog?

That's right, hmph, has such unmanly characteristics

How would you know if you've never spoken to him personally?

That's how it seems, how people say, what rumors portray.

Haven't you heard, he was at one point temporarily crazed, then
a group of guys got together to pull a prank on him, succeeded
in doing so, pushed him too much-was about to suicide

Rumor?

No, not this one, two people found him on time
and stopped him. The 'joke' wasn't even

Confide,

What do you mean?

It was done in a public event, where everyone had witnessed it.

Pitiful.. he wouldn't seem like someone who would let his guard
down-I mean he could be smarter than to come to that conclusion

Smart, that's one thing I'm sure is true. My brother had him in
his class last year, says the guy is all top grades, top comportment,
top liked – except for my brother of course, who is irked by
him. Says he's really some 'stuck up loser' covering it all up-

Meh, guess he's just a neutral player.

Even after hearing everything else, hearing yourself; you
still think that's the mere case…well I don't need you
anymore to tell me who he is, because I now know,

Oh yeah? Well then, who is he?

Poor fellow… just a help –needed young man- deep
down and to the core, a soul that is broken,

Disguised as a confident, kindly positive, valedictorian.

Heavy Lump

I'm feeling it again, here it comes,

I'm sensing it coming,

No, not this agonizing battle again, I fear to be tortured

I suppose… it cannot be helped

But endured

Heavy lump,

In my chest,

More than just a mere organ

That's job to pump life

Throughout me

Blackened;greyed, and heavy'ed by words uglier than a gorgon.

Let the fight begin-

My only defensive weapon, my heart,

I hope you can hold off the attack

I don't ask for a comeback,

Just sustain yourself patiently through the verbal thwack.

It begins...

Their weapons are strong,

Worse than I've expected

Of course most of them are just made of letters,

But today, there's more

Tangible, fiercer than any sword, powerful, more than any explosive

Oh, but what's this? What's this, this time? It
too, responds strongly, more than ever,

Lump grows larger, darkening,

In my chest in frenzy bumping

Wanting to come out to fight back in full presence

No, remain in place I say

No! I can't take it anymore, let me out It responds,

Hands on knees,

I bend over with the pain that comes from the pounding in my chest, It like a ball in a pinball machine

Oh no, It has a mind of its own, it is now undergoing bigotry,

Refusing to accede, and wanting to now avenge all the blackness and maleficent actions of antiquity.

But why react this way, why wish for that?

Do not be consumed by their darkness

It is unresponsive to my beseechingness

I quietly supplicate,

That it will all abate.

And so forth It continues

In wrath,

Powered by dark fiery fuel, initially put in there by the opposer's

Scath

It aims for the center, and pierce through, to try to come out

I straighten back up and slowly raise my hand up to my chest

In between my breasts

As if there was no flesh between me and It

But there isn't,

For it had already cut through, and is halfway out

And it can be seen now, but instead of being in different hues of pink

It lays on the edge of the hole it created, in black and grey.

Structured, and covered in layers of prickly
thorns, and wide silver blades.

I lay my hand over it, and put pressure on it.

My palm immediately sheds in crimson

And I wince, with an urge to scream piercing
throughout the rest of my body

And I think, better my hands than my life,

I must try to prevent you from falling out, are you
even sure you want to make this decision?

I lay my other hand on top of this one, and push
harder to try to put It back inside

The now matching red metacarpi slowly, but successfully push it in.

My body slowly leans backward and I start to fall

It might be back in, but all energy has flowed out

My eyes rolled back, I hit the ground with a loud 'thud'.

My vision came back into focus, but I just
continuously stare at the ceiling

and my eyes bleed tears,

but as each rolled down either side of my cheeks,

my lips form into a smile.

Because I can rest now.

I've made it through today's battle, and won today's fight

And can rest and sleep now,

For another 24 hours, the opposer's intended harm to me will shun

And I can sleep to rest now,

And it won't be an eternal one.

The Window and The Wall

A single window is on that wall

A single side, a single wall left,

from a dilapidated building

but on which secrets have been maintained and kept,

it tells stories of past historical events

things done to people that were then thought to be common

things done by people who did not have any repents

For you I feel sorry,

For the things you've endured, I think we share a common story,

As you've faced those who caused you to be marred,

I faced those whose words caused me to be scarred

Perhaps we are one…

as you look through the panels of your window,

that occasionally get misty and wet with dew

On behalf of us two…

You, wall, from the gloomy seasons, dark and black like tar

I, wall, from words that spread from afar

I, wall, try to speak up against them, but only drawl,

Tortured, like the thrall, that was once chained up to your wall

You, (the malevolent ones) yours; flagrant actions

I, wall, dismantled into fractions

But now, I've come to have the audacity to vent myself.

You, (the malevolent ones)

You've debased all things that were meant to be in a par,

But now I hope to have shown you what real words really are.

Unspoken Words

I have a voice,

but an inability to speak

however…

I might express things in a manner that is oblique.

Look into my eyes … they speak

hear my voice… it doesn't.

while I converse with you,

my insides churn uncomfortably with an irritated sensation

my mind too- starts to fill with frustration.

Because though my lips have finally moved,
the words that you have heard,

weren't the ones that I have intended.

In my mind-heart-and-soul, I really yelp;

wanting help to let it out

But any attempt to really do so, is a failure,
just as expected from any schlep.

Anxiety over-rules, and I end up sounding squeaky, drawly,
and vulnerable. I worry some of them for sounding like
I'm about to cry or blurt out something unexpected.

So the process and ability is much more difficult; distressing and
struggling just as someone whom accidently consumed ricin.

So when they day comes that I may finally speak,

All I ask from you,

Is to listen.

Subdued Soul

Across a meadow comes a doe

Where children had once played to-and-fro

Miles of trees under a blanket snow,

And silence pervades like the depths of sorrow

Puppet Scene

There is a room-

The temperature is neither cold, nor warm

The floor is neither rough or smooth,

And neither side of the walls allows you to decide
whether it is the front or back of the room.

It is dark, and the room is being watched upon. Light
only shines on where the scene plays out.

There-

A dresser stands. With a mirror.

A girl sits in a chair, watching her reflection.

She leans in as she starts to notice something unusual.

Something long and white is in the air, and it
seems to originate from her forearms.

She then looks away from the mirror, and down on her arms. They
were curled around her arms and seem to be injected into her skin
at the wrist. Only then did she also notice the wooden shackles.

Are these... like puppet strings? She wondered.

She looked down at her legs, and they had them too.

Suddenly anxious, she hurriedly stands up,
knocking the chair backward.

She looks up, but the puppet master is not visible. Only black emptiness.

But as she stared at it for a couple more seconds,
something started to reveal itself.

Grey sparkly letters glistened across a ceiling:

Lowercase m,f,t,a,s,

And Uppercase M&S.

Panic started to rise within the girl and she starts searching the
room frantically for something she can use to her advantage.

Then she has a glimpse of a small window on one of the windows.

What excited her was not the window itself,
but what lay on its window sill.

There laid a pair of large kitchen scissors.

Her strings were quite thin, surely they'll cut through, she thought.

She ran back to where the chair on the floor was,
picked it up, and went towards the window.

She climbed on top of the chair, extended her
right arm, and reached for the scissors.

However the ledge was still too high.

She stood on tiptoe, and stretched with all her might. She was a fingertip away.

When suddenly there was a strong yank that pulled her back. She fought it, and pulled forward, fighting all the vellications she felt in her body with all her might.

Almost clawing at the ledge, she finally reached the scissors, and snatched them.

Right then, a big sturdy jerk pulled at her and her strings, so powerfully, it caused her to fall off the chair; pulling her entire body at once, and dragging her across the floor, away from the window.

The girl looks up, to where her strings were being pulled from, and instead of the ceiling, there were black clouds. Large, swirling around in a circle, in an intimidating manner. As if a storm was stewing.

The girl looked at the hand that she used to supposedly clutch the scissors, but her palm was empty.

She had lost the scissors.

She looked at the wall, but the window disappeared.

She lowers her head as she admits failure, and sadly acknowledges her ascendance.

Mankind

A humanoid figure is in the room

is it a male or female? It doesn't matter, it is certainly a
person-from the view point on which it is looked upon

it sits on a throne-like chair-heavily decorated,
sparks and shines; color overload

across the forehead of the one who sits on it is the word: ***mankind***

a scrawny stubby man walks into the room.

He slowly and cautiously approaches *mankind*

In his hand is a silver tray with the globe on it.

when he reaches the throne, he kneels to one knee, lowers his head, raises
the tray above his head and offers it to *mankind* and says, " Here, sir."

But Mankind waves his hand in dismissal and says,
" No, bring it back to me in a *golden* tray."

Human Condition

I stand in the middle of nowhere

In each of my hands are two similar objects. I look at the right
hand and see that I'm holding an actual very live human heart.
Still pumping, very lightly, and veins and arteries of blue,
green and red running through it in zigzags and crosses

But what fascinated me the most was the fact that the light of imperial
gold shone around it in an enticing manner, beautifying the entire organ.

In the meantime, on my left hand, was an
unidentifiable object of supreme deformity.

It was completely covered in a hideous black gooey substance,
but judging from the feel of it, it seemed to be another heart. It
was also covered in a layer of thorns, and various trashy items
were stuck to it. The goo itself seemed to be in action, and was
melting onto my hand, yet not a single drop fell to the ground.

Further more, a red form of radiation was being emitted.

Next, I looked frontwards; to see what I will find in front of me.

According to my current vision, if what I saw was what really was,

Then there was a simple brick road; split into two pathways.

Again, the one on the left was the worst of the two; heavily polluted, grey smoke in the air, crooked and twisted, with a very dark and daunting forest at the end of pathway. But what was most frightening, was that there seemed to be ghost like figures floating around, and with washed away zombie faces and crimson shadows.

Moreover, I was shocked to see that some of them resembled, if not, had the very faces of my own relatives, and people I knew.

Knowing by then that the right side must hold something better, I turn to the right.

Sure enough, the road itself seemed better. It was perfectly straight and immaculate.

I could not see where its destination would lead to, but could only see a shiny golden foam ahead, along with puffy white clouds that looked like giant marshmallows.

A few healthy and pleasant looking citizens were walking across the path, and each and every one of them wore beautiful green garments, with elaborate colorful jewelry for both the men and the woman. I was relieved to see some familiar faces among them.

I was urged to take that path, but as I came to raise my feet, I found that I could not. I looked down and saw that on each ankle, there was a heavy black chain glued to the ground.

Chords that I did not notice before, attached those shackles to both of the hearts in my hands.

Not that I wanted to go there, but just to test my mobility, I turn and lean my body towards the left. But when I tried to walk, I also couldn't go there.

I might as well have been paralyzed, because I felt stuck and confused. I look at the two hearts in my hands, and wonder what is their importance, for surely they play a role in my limitations.

Then an idea struck me. If neither one of them would individually allow me to go anywhere, then perhaps an intermediate form of the two would.

So I raised my arms, rotate my hands so that their surfaces would face each other, and quickly squished the two together. Red, orange, and yellow sparks exploded out of my hands. Then green, blue and purple hues glowed.

When the -morphism was over, I open my hands to find an average human heart, with nothing quite particular about it, with a plain pinkish colour.

I then looked up to see what I would see in front of me. The paths too, have merged into one.

It was now a simple brick road, neither perfectly straight, nor did it seem wobbly and full of zigzags. I lifted my legs, and found that I could walk again. So I walked towards it.

As for the heart, I lifted it up towards my chest, and my shirt opened up in the center; my skin too, opening a hole, painlessly, and I delicately placed it inside.

Then something flashed before me, as if someone simply clicked on the lights. I realized it was my eyesight; accommodating itself with the changes.

I walked on… seeing regular humans dressed casually, some walking fine, some limping, all seemingly following the same path I was taking.

I wondered what I would encounter along the way, and worried
that my vision might deceive me, but finally understood I had
a tool to guide me. It was what I recently put inside of me.

I took comfort in the fact that I was meant to be here, and knew, that
it would, for the most part, rely on how I decided to deal with it. That
will result on the consequences of where I will go and what I see.

Humming bird; pretty

Humming bird; pretty.

Humming bird flies round circle

’till humming no more.

What is Succes?

There are two kinds of success

There is that-

that can be pertained academically,

that- of- the one,

perhaps in your career,

among other things.

But there is also that of life.

How do you know if you've achieved it?

Well that depends on each individual's unique standpoint in their life

Take my mother for example,

she claims to have not reached success yet,

what it is for her,

is when the day will arrive that she has seen all her children grown up, done well in their paths of life, live well in their homes, and happily with their respective spouses.

That for her, is when she'll be satiated

as a parent, and as an individual

that is her-succeeding. Untill then, she isn't sure she is successful.

Perhaps it's when you've finally felt like you've
done what you were set out to do,

Or maybe when you've realized a dream

As a student, educator, parent, employee…

Or whatever the case may be..

Ask your own parents, friends, and fellow colleagues,

What is for them to have success?

Ever felt degraded at some point, surrounded with people or a
particular person who seems to have gotten it all, while you're behind,
completed a task, achieved a goal, and/or merely successful,

Will *are* they really?

Or was it something they had merely done in a certain field of activity.?

So who's the one that is really going to succeed
here, at the end of the road?

And as for you? What is it for you-

success?

Life

L ots of phases, -

I intricate

F orever to be understood and will-

E nd one day.

What Is That- Beyond Us?

The heavens above us is an interesting entity

Pondered about in all forms, throughout antiquity

And in all humanity alike, - sisterhoods and fraternity

To the degree, bringing about the questioning of one's identity

Its very makings, intertwined with the flowing current of the soul

Fascinations of the galaxies, and inspirations that we deem our own

Bright star, an explosion of colour-nebulae,

and what is that- that feeling swarming in and around us like vespidae?

A fleeting feeling, composed of human emotions, beaming-

Sparkles it way across the globe, to those
who reject it, or find it appealing

Some confused, and fearing, while others find it freeing

And to most, are embraced and comforted by
the thought of the author of our being

www.ingramcontent.com/pod-product-compliance
Ingram Content Group UK Ltd.
Pitfield, Milton Keynes, MK11 3LW, UK
UKHW020137250726
13967UKWH00002B/712